POLLUTING THE AIR

*First published in
the United States in 1992 by*
Gloucester Press Inc.
95 Madison Ave
New York, NY 10016

Library of Congress Cataloging-in-Publication Data

Hare, Tony.
    Polluting the air / by Tony Hare.
        p. cm. -- (Save our earth)
    Includes index.
    Summary: Examines the causes and effects of
air pollution and explores methods to combat
this threat.
    ISBN 0-531-17346-1
    1. Air--Pollution--Juvenile literature. 2.
Automobiles--Pollution control devices--Juvenile
literature. 3. Renewable energy sources--Juvenile
literature. [1. Air--Pollution. 2. Pollution.] I. Title.
II. Series: Hare, Tony. Save our earth.
TD883.13.H37   1992
363.73'92--dc20   91-34101   CIP   AC

Printed in Belgium

The publishers would like to
acknowledge that the
photographs reproduced within
this book have been posed by
models or have been obtained
from photographic agencies.

Design   David West
                  Children's Book
                  Design
Designer   Steve Woosnam-Savage
Editor   Elise Bradbury
Picture research Emma Krikler
Illustrator   Ian Moores

The author, Dr. Tony Hare, is a
writer, ecologist and television
presenter. He works with several
environmental organizations, including
the London Wildlife Trust, the
British Association of Nature
Conservationists, and Plantlife, of
which he is chairman of the board.

The consultants: Dr. Claire Holman
is an environmental consultant
specializing in air pollution.

Jacky Karas works for Friends of the
Earth. Prior to this she was a Senior
Research Associate at the Climatic
Research Unit at the University of
East Anglia. She also operates as an
independent environmental consultant.

SAVE OUR EARTH

POLLUTING THE AIR

TONY HARE

GLOUCESTER PRESS

New York · London · Toronto · Sydney

CONTENTS

INTRODUCTION

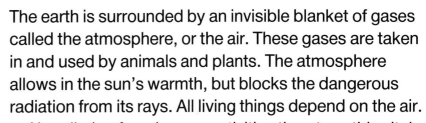

The earth is surrounded by an invisible blanket of gases called the atmosphere, or the air. These gases are taken in and used by animals and plants. The atmosphere allows in the sun's warmth, but blocks the dangerous radiation from its rays. All living things depend on the air.

Air pollution from human activities threatens this vital resource. Exhaust fumes from cars and emissions from industries pour into the air, making cities unliveable. The air in Mexico City is so polluted that oxygen is sold on the streets. Even the rain has been contaminated by pollution in many parts of the world.

There are hundreds of kinds of air pollutants, some of which can seriously threaten health. Even chemicals that do not harm people can alter the balance of gases in the atmosphere. The result could be global temperature changes and a loss of the protection the atmosphere's gases provide for the planet.

In most of the industrialized world, the air is cleaner now than it was 50 years ago. This is because methods were found that reduce the amount of pollution released into the air. Researchers continue to develop solutions, like cars that produce less exhaust fumes. We must encourage these steps in order to prevent air pollution from doing any further damage.

◄ **A common feature of cities is the smog which hangs over their skylines. But the pollution which swirls around Arizona's Grand Canyon is a shocking example of the extent of the problem. The smog is caused by a coal-burning power plant 80 miles away. However, the future looks brighter. The offending power plant is to cut the amount of gases it releases by 90 percent.**

THE AIR AROUND US

The air is a mixture of gases. Nitrogen is the main gas, making up 78 percent of the atmosphere. Oxygen is also abundant, accounting for another 21 percent. Two gases that are essential to life, carbon dioxide and ozone, occur in quantities of less than 1 percent. Ozone is a pale blue gas which is poisonous if breathed in. Yet high in the atmosphere it forms a shield that protects the earth from harmful radiation from the sun.

The way carbon dioxide passes between animals and plants is a good example of how the atmosphere's gases are used by living things. As humans and other animals breathe in oxygen and exhale carbon dioxide, plants take in carbon dioxide and produce oxygen. This pattern of recycling helps to ensure that the air maintains the right balance of gases for all forms of life.

Pollution adds certain gases to the atmosphere and breaks down others, changing the fragile balance of the air. Gases like carbon monoxide can harm human health if large amounts are inhaled. Other gases are harmless to people, but damage the environment.

▶ Scientists divide the atmosphere into layers. The layer closest to earth is called the troposphere. Weather occurs here. The next layer is the stratosphere, where long distance jets fly. The air gets thinner upward through the atmosphere, until outer space begins, where there is no air at all.

◀ This satellite photo shows the familiar outline of Africa, and the vast oceans and cloud formations of our planet. Without the atmosphere, the earth's surface would be completely different. The moon, which does not have a protective atmosphere, has a rocky, cratered landscape where nothing lives.

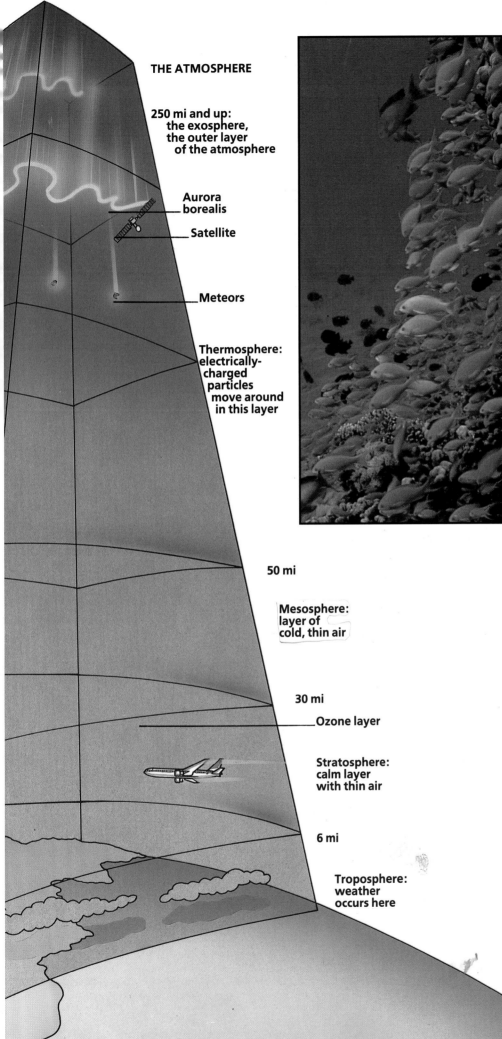

THE ATMOSPHERE

250 mi and up:
the exosphere,
the outer layer
of the atmosphere

Aurora borealis

Satellite

Meteors

Thermosphere:
electrically-
charged
particles
move around
in this layer

50 mi

Mesosphere:
layer of
cold, thin air

30 mi

Ozone layer

Stratosphere:
calm layer
with thin air

6 mi

Troposphere:
weather
occurs here

▲ The atmosphere affects all things on earth, even life in the oceans. Although they may never touch the air, the plants and animals in the seas owe their existence to it. Like life on land, they depend on oxygen and carbon dioxide, which dissolve in the water. The atmosphere even plays an important role in keeping the oceans full of water. The air contains water vapor which falls to the earth as rain and snow, keeping the oceans full. Some of the seawater evaporates back into the air, continually recycling itself. The earth is the only known planet with water, which is essential to life.

POLLUTING THE AIR

When a substance gets into the environment in sufficiently large quantities to cause damage, it is called a pollutant. Air pollution comes in many forms. The most serious pollution comes from human-made sources.

There are two main reasons for this. The first is that our activities produce far more pollution than nature can easily cope with. Volcanoes emit the same gas, sulfur dioxide, as coal-burning power plants. But volcanoes rarely erupt and are scattered around the world, whereas power plants belch out gases continually.

The second problem is that substances have been developed which do not exist in nature. They can do a lot of damage because nothing exists to break them down.

**SOURCES OF
AIR POLLUTION**

Nuclear power plants
Although very rare, a handful of accidents at nuclear power plants have occurred, releasing above-average levels of radiation.

Metal smelters
Gases from smelters can carry heavy metals, which can cause mental disorders if received in large doses.

Oil rigs and refineries
Burning surplus gas produces pollution which can form acid rain. Refineries emit chemicals that can cause cancer.

Cars and airplanes
Burning gasoline releases gases that combine in sunlight to create ozone, which is poisonous at ground level. Cars can also emit lead particles which can cause brain damage.

Cities
Factories, cars and home fires produce a mixture of harmful air pollution.

Coal power plants
Burning coal releases gases like sulfur dioxide, which causes acid rain.

◄ Air pollution comes from a range of sources. It can result in a local problem, like smogs in cities. It can also affect a wider area, as the wind carries gases far from their source. Now pollution is also recognized as a problem which affects the planet, since it could be changing the atmosphere.

Garbage dump
Rotting food scraps produce methane. Burning waste can release many different gases; some of these can make the eyes burn.

Chemical plants
Release poisonous gases like chlorine and formaldehyde, which can damage the eyes, nose and lungs.

Farming
Farmers spray chemicals called pesticides and fertilizers over crops. These can drift with the wind and harm people and wildlife.

► Lightning is a natural source of air pollution. Every year it produces 100 million tons of gases called oxides of nitrogen, which can cause acid rain. This is equal to the amount human sources produce. However, lightning occurs all around the world, so the gases can be dispersed.

POLLUTION FROM ENERGY

Energy is what powers most of the things that are part of our everyday lives. Energy supplies light and heat, it runs cars and trains, it cooks our food and powers our appliances. The main way we generate energy is by burning coal, oil, and gas. These resources, called fossil fuels, are the remains of prehistoric plants and animals which lay buried in the ground for millions of years.

Burning fossil fuels produces air pollution. Fossil fuels contain the carbon dioxide that the once-living plants and animals absorbed. When they are burned, this gas is released. It is harmless to humans, but in the atmosphere it traps heat. Worldwide, billions of tons of fossil fuels are burned each year, and the carbon dioxide released could disrupt the climate (see page 18).

Other polluting gases are also produced when fossil fuels are burned. Sulfur dioxide and oxides of nitrogen are the main gases that cause acid rain. Over 85 percent of these gases come from burning fossil fuels.

▼ During the Gulf War of 1991, hundreds of Kuwaiti oil wells were set alight. The result was an extreme example of what burning fossil fuels does to the environment. Satellite pictures showed great black clouds engulfing the country. The smoke plunged Kuwait into darkness during daytime, and produced polluting gases at a rate as fast as all the power plants in Britain put together.

◄ Power plants that burn coal to make electricity are some of the worst polluters. Coal produces more carbon dioxide when it is burned than any other fuel. It also produces more sulfur dioxide. Power plants in poor areas, like Eastern Europe, China, and India (shown here) rely on brown coal. It is cheaper than hard coal, but it is the dirtiest when it is burned. The result is that these areas are some of the most blighted by pollution. Other fuels used in power plants, like orimulsion, made from tarry sand, also pollute the air.

Nuclear power provides electricity for many countries. It is often viewed as "clean" energy because it does not rely on burning fossil fuels. Nuclear power plants create energy by splitting atoms, which produces radioactivity. Large doses of certain kinds of radioactivity can damage living things. Nuclear power plants release small amounts of radioactivity into the atmosphere during normal operations. Radioactivity is invisible; what you see pouring from the towers of this German nuclear power station is mainly steam. But many people are concerned that aging reactors might develop leaks which would let out dangerous levels of radioactivity.

SMOGGY CITIES

Smog plagues many cities, from Bombay, where breathing the air is equivalent to smoking 10 cigarettes a day, to Benxi in China, which recently disappeared from satellite photos under a thick cloud of air pollution.

Smog (smoky fog) is a mixture of air pollution, including sulfur and nitrogen oxides, carbon monoxide, and other gases released by factories, cars, and power plants. On their own, some of these pollutants can cause burning eyes, breathing problems and even cancer. In the air over cities, they can also combine to form other dangerous types of pollution.

There are two types of smog. One type, called reducing smog, occurs as a result of a large number of small fires in people's homes. The smoke from the fires combines with pollution from industry to form smog, especially in cold weather. The other type of smog, photochemical smog, is caused mainly by car exhausts.

▼ **The 550 million vehicles in the world are the main cause of the gases that create smog. In Athens, exhaust pollution can get so bad that the city has to ban cars from the center.**

▶ **Los Angeles is the city of smog. Its residents mainly use cars for transportation. Those living in the most polluted areas of the city may suffer lung problems as a result of the smog.**

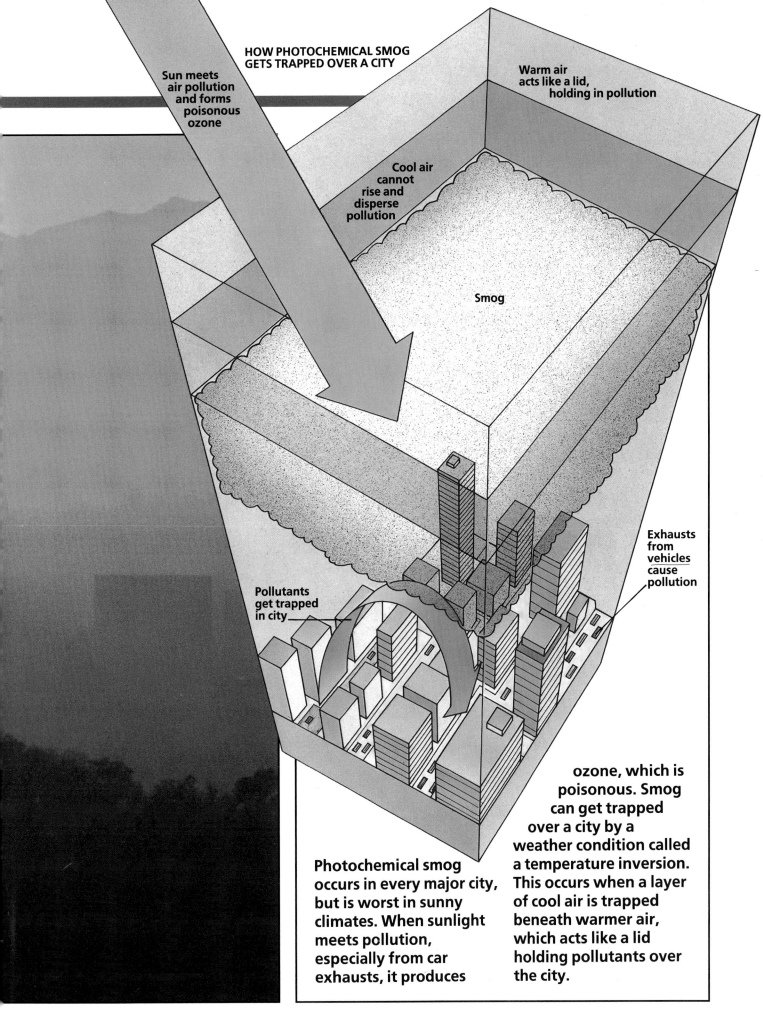

HOW PHOTOCHEMICAL SMOG GETS TRAPPED OVER A CITY

Sun meets air pollution and forms poisonous ozone

Warm air acts like a lid, holding in pollution

Cool air cannot rise and disperse pollution

Smog

Exhausts from vehicles cause pollution

Pollutants get trapped in city

Photochemical smog occurs in every major city, but is worst in sunny climates. When sunlight meets pollution, especially from car exhausts, it produces ozone, which is poisonous. Smog can get trapped over a city by a weather condition called a temperature inversion. This occurs when a layer of cool air is trapped beneath warmer air, which acts like a lid holding pollutants over the city.

POISONED COUNTRYSIDE

Cities are not the only places that suffer problems from the air pollution they produce. The wind carries pollutants far from their source, affecting farms, the countryside, and even the wilderness.

Acid rain is one example. It is produced when oxides of sulfur and nitrogen from burning fossil fuels or wood combine with water in the air. Clouds can carry the acidic water long distances before it falls.

Acid rain poisons lakes by making the water acidic. When it falls on trees and plants it damages their leaves and releases dangerous substances from the soil where they grow. Germany and the Netherlands have had half their forests damaged by acid rain. Scandinavian countries bear the brunt of pollution carried from Britain. Acid rain has killed the fish in 80 percent of their lakes. In the eastern United States, thousands of lakes are too acidic for fish to live in them.

Human health is also affected by acid rain. People living near where it falls can inhale dangerous amounts, and suffer lung complaints.

HOW ACID RAIN IS FORMED

Wind carries pollutants until they meet moisture in clouds.

Oxides of sulfur and nitrogen rise up from chimneys of coal power plants.

Nitrogen oxides drift up from vehicle exhausts.

◄ **To keep their crops from being damaged by pests, farmers spray chemicals called pesticides on their fields. These poisons kill the pests. However, the wind can carry the spray away where it can harm wildlife and even people.**

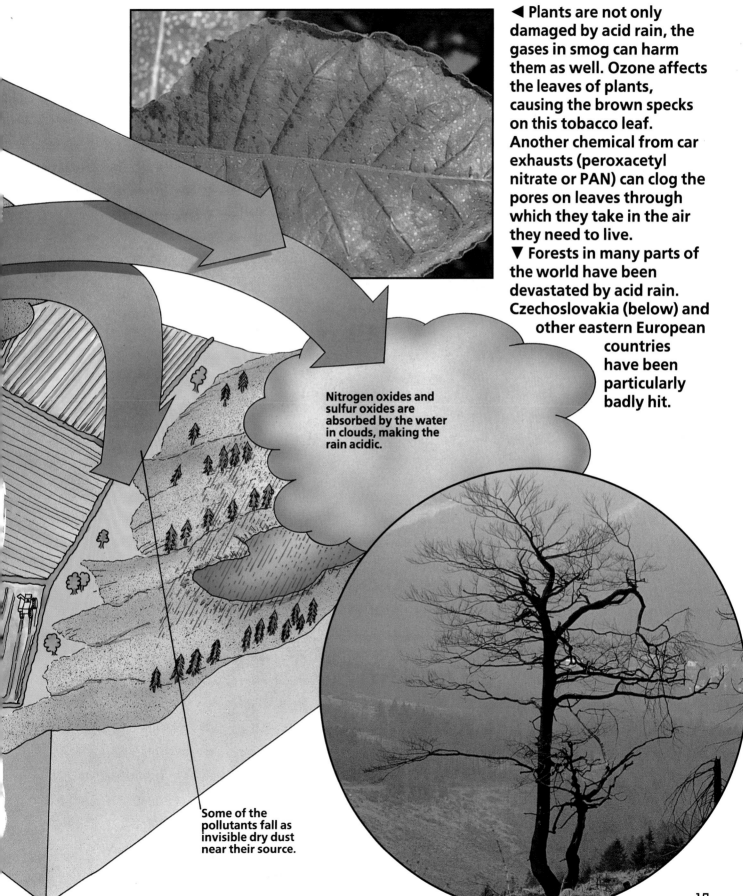

◄ Plants are not only damaged by acid rain, the gases in smog can harm them as well. Ozone affects the leaves of plants, causing the brown specks on this tobacco leaf. Another chemical from car exhausts (peroxacetyl nitrate or PAN) can clog the pores on leaves through which they take in the air they need to live.

▼ Forests in many parts of the world have been devastated by acid rain. Czechoslovakia (below) and other eastern European countries have been particularly badly hit.

Nitrogen oxides and sulfur oxides are absorbed by the water in clouds, making the rain acidic.

Some of the pollutants fall as invisible dry dust near their source.

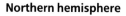

Northern hemisphere

◄▼ These maps show the extent of ozone destruction during the 1980s. Antarctica has had the largest decline in ozone levels. The southern tip of South America is also losing its ozone protection. By 1989, ozone levels were decreasing over North America and Europe. Scientists now claim that ozone reduction over Europe has been greater than was originally thought.

Ozone depletion

- 1.5% loss
- 3 % loss
- 4.5 % loss
- 6 % loss
- 7.5 % loss
- 9 % loss
- No measurement available

Southern hemisphere

▼ The oceans around Antarctica contain tiny plants and animals called plankton. Many sea creatures rely on plankton for food. An excess of radiation from the sun could disrupt the breeding of plankton and upset the ocean food chain.

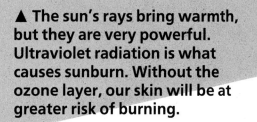

▲ The sun's rays bring warmth, but they are very powerful. Ultraviolet radiation is what causes sunburn. Without the ozone layer, our skin will be at greater risk of burning.

THE OZONE HOLE

Life on our planet relies on a layer of ozone gas high in the atmosphere. Ozone absorbs dangerous ultraviolet radiation from the sun which could damage plants and animals, including people, if it reached the earth.

In 1985, scientists discovered that the amount of ozone over Antarctica had decreased significantly. The "hole" in the ozone layer was found to be caused by certain kinds of pollution, in particular, by chemicals called CFCs (chlorofluorocarbons). CFCs are gases used to keep refrigerators and air conditioners cool, and are also used in some aerosols and foam packaging. As they drift through the atmosphere, the sun's rays cause them to release chlorine, which destroys ozone.

The ozone hole is getting bigger, posing a serious threat. It has been estimated that a 1 percent depletion of the ozone layer could result in a 2 percent increase in cases of skin cancer, which already causes 100,000 deaths a year. Plants can also be harmed by exposure to radiation, which can reduce leaf size and stunt growth. Unfortunately, the ozone which does so much damage at ground level cannot drift up to reinforce the ozone layer in the atmosphere.

▼ CFCs have many different uses. For years they were used in aerosol cans to help propel the contents out of the can when it was sprayed. Since CFCs' ability to destroy the ozone layer was discovered, many countries have banned them from use in aerosols. However, they continue to be used in air conditioners, foam and refrigerators. CFCs are very long-lasting and can drift through the stratosphere for up to 100 years, so the gas already there could still be destroying ozone a century from now.

Increasing the Greenhouse Effect

Over the last century, the earth's average temperature has risen by about 1°F. Some scientists believe this might be due to increasing levels of greenhouse gases, like carbon dioxide, which is very effective at trapping heat. If our power plants, cars and factories keep releasing greenhouse gases at the current rate, by 2050 we could make the world hotter than it has been for 10,000 years.

Some of the heat from the earth escapes back to space.

Some of the heat from the earth is trapped by gases in the atmosphere, known as greenhouse gases.

Heat from the sun warms the earth.

Methane is an explosive gas produced by rotting waste, burning vegetation and rice paddies. It makes a large contribution to trapping heat

CFCs are very effective greenhouse gases. They leak from scrapped refrigerators, air conditioners and some types of foam packaging.

Ozone, a product of photochemical smog in cities, also traps heat.

Burning fossil fuels in cars, factories and power plants produces carbon dioxide, which traps heat. Cars also release other heat-trappers, for example, nitrous oxides.

GLOBAL WARMING

The atmosphere makes life possible by keeping the planet warm. The sun's rays pass through to warm the earth, then certain gases like carbon dioxide and water vapor trap the heat as it is given off by the earth's surface. This is called the Greenhouse Effect, because the gases act like the glass in a greenhouse. Without it, the planet would be about 54°F colder.

Air pollution is increasing the amount of gases that trap heat in the atmosphere. Scientists fear this is raising the world's temperature, a process known as global warming, and that this could disrupt the climate.

The late 1980s brought some of the worst droughts and hottest summers ever known to North America and other parts of the world. In 1991, Australia suffered the worst drought in recorded history. No one can be sure that global warming was the cause, but if it is, worse things may be yet to come. Disrupting the climate could affect the growth of crops and melt the polar ice caps, flooding low-lying areas like the Nile Delta.

▼ **Burning tropical rainforests may be increasing global warming. These ancient forests have been taking in carbon dioxide for millions of years. Today the rainforests are being cleared at an incredible rate for farming and cattle ranching. Such vast tracts of forest are burned that the smoke can be seen from space. When trees are burned, carbon dioxide is released. Forest burning may contribute up to a third of the carbon dioxide being added to the atmosphere by people.**

Burning the Amazon rainforest in Brazil

19

OTHER POLLUTANTS

Many of our activities poison the air. All over the world, billions of tons of chemicals are released into the atmosphere every year from a huge variety of industries.

Smelters, where rocks are heated to separate metals from their rock ore, release heavy metals into the air. Lead, nickel and cadmium can all be produced during smelting, and each is very harmful to health. Lead can damage the nervous system, and can cause mental disabilities in growing children.

Cars that use leaded gasoline also release particles of lead with their exhaust fumes. Unleaded gasoline is being encouraged by many countries to stop this unnecessary source of dangerous pollution.

Benzene is another harmful air pollutant. It is a cancer-causing substance, and is found in crude oil and in gasoline. It is released into the air from oil refineries, vehicle exhausts, car gas tanks and filling stations.

▼ Incinerators burn garbage and hazardous waste at high temperatures. This reduces the amount of waste and destroys some dangerous substances. However, burning can produce harmful chemicals as well. Highly poisonous compounds called dioxins are produced when some plastics are burned. Incinerators, like this one in Rotterdam, have strict controls on what they release to the air. However, some incinerators are less efficient and high levels of dioxins have been found near them.

▶ Accidents can result in fatal kinds of air pollution. In 1984, a cloud of poisonous gas escaped from a pesticide factory at Bhopal in India, resulting in the worst pollution incident in history. At least 2,500 people died that day, and thousands more died in later years.

◀ Many normal workplace activities pollute the air. Paint can contain chemicals called solvents. People who inhale large amounts of solvents complain of headaches and nausea.

▲ This US train carrying toxic chemicals caught fire, releasing its chemicals to the air. From 1980-1985, 7,000 accidents releasing toxic substances occurred in the United States.

CLEANING THE AIR

The industrialized world has taken measures to clean the air. Many governments demand that power plants install scrubbers; devices in smokestacks that remove sulfur dioxide from gases before they are released.

Most new cars are designed to run on unleaded gas. Catalytic converters can be fitted to car exhausts to reduce nitrogen oxides and other pollutants. The United States requires catalytic converters on all new cars, and from 1992, the EC will enforce a similar law.

In 1989, the governments of 81 countries agreed to gradually stop the use of CFCs, in an attempt to protect the ozone layer. International talks to limit carbon dioxide emissions were underway in 1991/92.

However, even as progress is made in some areas, in others, steps are taken back. Poor regions, like eastern Europe, Asia, and Africa, cannot afford pollution controls. Even the wealthier countries are often reluctant to introduce costly pollution-control technology. There is much that remains for us to do to clean up the air.

▼ City governments have tackled pollution from car exhausts in a variety of ways. In Florence, Italy, traffic is banned from the city center during daylight hours. Amsterdam relies on electric streetcars, which release no fumes where they run. Pollution is produced by the power plants which generate the electricity they run on, but streetcars are still far cleaner than cars. Bicycles create no pollution at all.

Electric trams in Amsterdam keep the city center free from exhaust fumes.

Many people around the world rely on bicycles as their main form of transportation.

Manufacturing goods from recycled materials reduces air pollution. Making glass goods from recycled glass can cut up to 20 percent of the air pollution generated in making glass goods from scratch.

This Kenyan home uses the sun's energy to provide hot water, producing no pollution.

► Reducing our reliance on fossil fuels to provide energy is the main priority in cleaning up the air. Iceland provides heat for all the residents of its capital city with geothermal power plants (right). Geothermal power uses hot rocks under the earth's surface to make electricity. This produces no carbon dioxide. However, geothermal energy is only possible where hot rocks are near the surface. Also, precautions must be taken to prevent certain harmful gases from escaping into the air with the steam.

A BETTER FUTURE?

Concern for the welfare of the planet is growing. The state of California has declared that by 2003, 10 percent of cars must emit virtually no exhaust fumes.

Electricity can be provided by resources that produce little air pollution. These include the waves, tides, wind, and the sun. Most of these methods of generating electricity are only possible in certain places. Tidal power, for example, relies on coastal areas with a wide variation in tides, like northern France. Solar power works best in regions which are sunny all year round. A combination of different forms of energy production could be used to suit particular areas.

There are even ways we can use potential air pollution to provide energy. Methane gas from rotting waste is a greenhouse gas. Pioneering schemes at landfills in North America and Europe now collect methane and convert it to electricity by burning it.

CITY OF THE FUTURE

Smaller cars which run on clean fuel (see page 29). No cars will be allowed in the city center. Battery-run buses create no emissions where they run.

Streetcars to carry people into the center, producing no fumes in the city itself.

◄ This is one of three Californian wind farms which together generate 90 percent of the world's wind-generated electricity. California is hoping to expand its wind energy production. The Netherlands also has plans for a large wind farm.

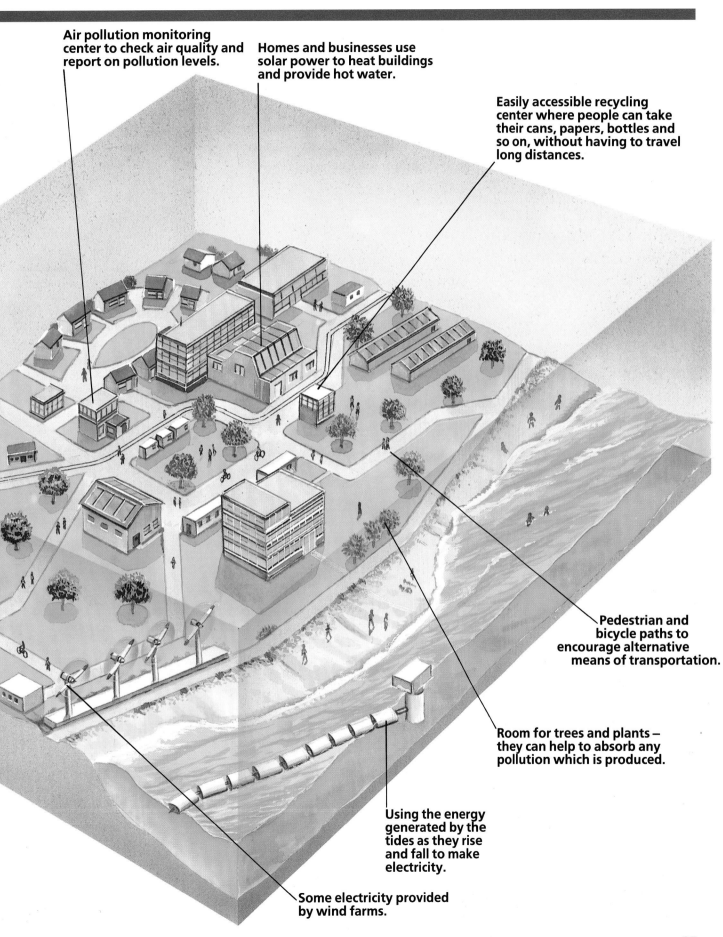

Air pollution monitoring center to check air quality and report on pollution levels.

Homes and businesses use solar power to heat buildings and provide hot water.

Easily accessible recycling center where people can take their cans, papers, bottles and so on, without having to travel long distances.

Pedestrian and bicycle paths to encourage alternative means of transportation.

Room for trees and plants – they can help to absorb any pollution which is produced.

Using the energy generated by the tides as they rise and fall to make electricity.

Some electricity provided by wind farms.

WHAT YOU CAN DO

You can help to reduce air pollution:
- Be aware of saving energy, and turn off lights and heat when they are not necessary.
- Use public transportation, walk or ride a bicycle when you can. Cars are the most polluting form of transport.
- Avoid using aerosol sprays. Even if aerosols do not contain CFCs, the substitutes for CFCs used in spray cans can also harm the ozone layer.
- Recycle or reuse goods when you have finished with them, because manufacturing creates air pollution.

Useful addresses:

Acid Rain Foundation
1630 Blackhawk Hills
St. Paul, MN 55122

Friends of the Earth
530 Seventh Street, S.E.
Washington, DC 20003

Air Pollution Control Association
P.O. Box 2861
Pittsburgh, PA 15340

National Clean Air Coalition
801 Pennsylvania Avenue, S.E.
Washington, DC 20003

Designing a poster:

One of the most important things that can be done is to make more people aware of the dangers of air pollution. One way you can do this is to make a poster to hang up at school.

1) Think up a striking and clever heading for the poster which will grab the attention of people passing by.

2) Design an illustration or symbol like the one shown here or cut pictures out of magazines and make a collage that conveys the main theme.

3) Read through this book and try to summarize in about 30-40 words why air pollution poses a health threat and why it is causing problems that could be with us for many generations to come.

4) Again by reading through the book, make some suggestions as to how we can solve the problems of air pollution.

5) Include some other information if there is room, such as useful addresses to contact for more information.

POISONED AIR

CHOKING SMOGS POLLUTE OUR CITIES, FACTORIES, CARS, AND POWER PLANTS PUMP OUT DANGEROUS CHEMICALS. THE AIR IS BECOMING UNFIT TO BREATHE IN SOME AREAS. POLLUTION TODAY ALSO AFFECTS THE EARTH'S FUTURE. WE ARE CHANGING THE BALANCE OF NATURE BY RELEASING POLLUTING GASES.

WHAT CAN YOU DO?
- WALK OR RIDE A BICYCLE WHENEVER POSSIBLE.
- CONSERVE ENERGY BY TURNING OFF LIGHTS AND HEATING WHEN THEY ARE NOT NECESSARY.
- AVOID USING AEROSOLS WITH CFCs.

USEFUL ADDRESSES

FACT FILE 1

Noise pollution

Jackhammers, car alarms, emergency sirens and loud music all contribute to noise pollution, which can damage hearing. One out of ten people in urban areas is exposed to harmful levels of noise every day. Better planning can help ease the problem, for example, if airports are built away from where people live and work.

Air pollution hotspots

The boys below breathe in the most polluted air in the world. Behind them, a factory belches yet more noxious gases into the air. They live in Cubato, Brazil, a town so blighted by pollution that no birds or insects live there. In 32 European cities, the air is officially deemed a health hazard. Eastern European cities are particularly affected by severe air pollution. Recent studies of Hungary show that air pollution is directly or indirectly responsible for one out of every 17 deaths.

Cures for global warming

The best way to combat global warming is for governments to encourage methods of producing energy other than burning fossil fuels. There are also ways to reduce the amount of carbon dioxide already in the air. One way is by growing more plants. Plants absorb carbon dioxide, so the more plants there are, the less chance of global warming. However, to make a significant difference, vast numbers of trees would have to be planted. Some scientists have also put forward more bizarre ideas to prevent global warming. Suggestions range from installing shields in space to reflect the sun's rays away from earth, to growing huge floating forests of waterplants on the oceans, which would absorb carbon dioxide. One proposal involves a fleet of 700 jets that would fly around the world every day, spraying artificial particles into the stratosphere to reflect the sun's rays back to space.

Alternative fuels

Research into fuels other than gasoline to run cars is growing. One reason for this is that oil reserves are limited and may only last only another 50 years. Also, cars which produce cleaner exhaust fumes are becoming more desirable. Methanol fuel, a type of alcohol made from plants, has been one of the most successful. Car manufacturers have experimented with cars run on methanol, like this Chevrolet model (left). At the moment, methanol cars are not as efficient as gasoline-run cars, and although their exhaust fumes are quite clean, they still produce harmful gases. Hydrogen is also being researched as a future fuel. When it is burned it mainly releases water vapor. European governments and car manufacturers like BMW have recently launched research into hydrogen-powered buses and lorries. The test-runs on these vehicles have been promising.

The nuclear dream?

Although nuclear power is heralded by some as the energy of the future, it does have disadvantages. One problem is that it produces radioactive waste, which cannot be destroyed and has to be stored for a very long time before it is safe. Scientists are trying to solve this dilemma by developing a form of nuclear power called fusion. This involves atoms joining together instead of splitting apart, and creates far less radioactive waste. In 1991, a breakthrough was made by scientists at a fusion reactor like the one below. However, using fusion to provide electricity will not be a reality for at least 50 years.

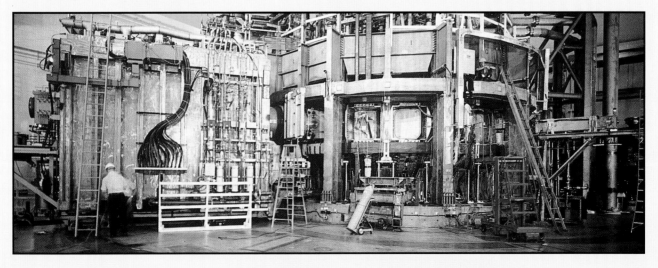

FACT FILE 2

Pollution in the home

People spend up to 90 percent of their time indoors, so air pollution in the home, school or workplace can be a real problem. In recent years, the air inside some buildings has been found to be more dangerous than polluted air outside. Certain buildings, especially where windows cannot be opened to let in fresh air, are affected by "sick building syndrome." Indoor air pollution is believed to contribute to sick building syndrome. Air pollutants can cause dizziness, headaches, coughing, sneezing, or drowsiness.

Cigarette smoke is one of the worst types of indoor air pollution. It can cause lung cancer if it is inhaled. It can also contribute to breathing problems for people with sensitive lungs, like those who suffer from asthma. Fresh paint releases fumes indoors, as do some kinds of insulation. Sprays like air fresheners or germ killers can also pollute indoor air. The best way to control the pollution inside buildings is to allow fresh air in. Some types of house plants, like spider plants, also help to purify the air by absorbing toxic chemicals.

INDOOR AIR POLLUTANTS

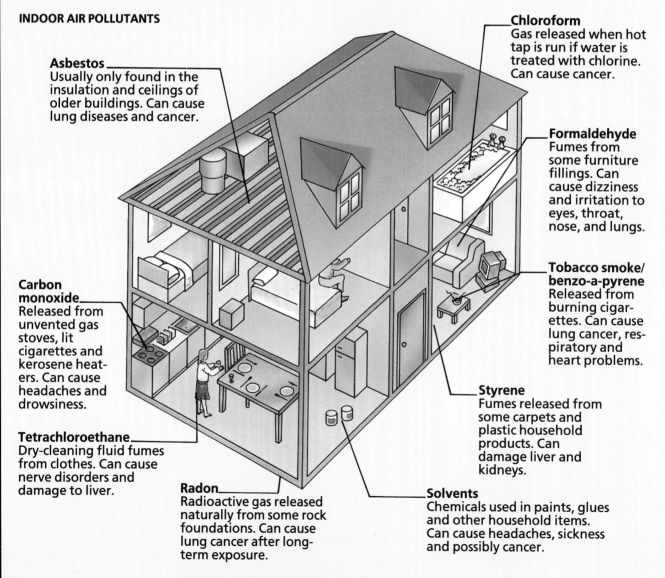

Asbestos
Usually only found in the insulation and ceilings of older buildings. Can cause lung diseases and cancer.

Chloroform
Gas released when hot tap is run if water is treated with chlorine. Can cause cancer.

Formaldehyde
Fumes from some furniture fillings. Can cause dizziness and irritation to eyes, throat, nose, and lungs.

Carbon monoxide
Released from unvented gas stoves, lit cigarettes and kerosene heaters. Can cause headaches and drowsiness.

Tobacco smoke/ benzo-a-pyrene
Released from burning cigarettes. Can cause lung cancer, respiratory and heart problems.

Tetrachloroethane
Dry-cleaning fluid fumes from clothes. Can cause nerve disorders and damage to liver.

Styrene
Fumes released from some carpets and plastic household products. Can damage liver and kidneys.

Radon
Radioactive gas released naturally from some rock foundations. Can cause lung cancer after long-term exposure.

Solvents
Chemicals used in paints, glues and other household items. Can cause headaches, sickness and possibly cancer.

GLOSSARY

Acid rain – weak acids are substances that are sharp to the taste, like vinegar and lemon juice. Strong acids, like sulfuric that contains sulfur, can dissolve stone, burn metal, and destroy living things. Acid rain is caused when chemicals produced by burning fossil fuels, especially oxides of sulfur and nitrogen, combine with water in clouds.

CFCs (chlorofluorocarbons) – long-lasting chemicals used in many products, including aerosols, refrigerators and air-conditioning systems. When refrigerators are scrapped, or aerosols are sprayed, CFCs are released into the air and float slowly up through the atmosphere. There the sun's radiation breaks them down into chlorine, which destroys ozone in the ozone layer. CFCs are now being phased out.

Emissions – substances like gases or liquids that are released (emitted) into the environment.

Global warming – the earth stays warm through a process called the Greenhouse Effect, whereby gases in the atmosphere trap heat. But when gases like carbon dioxide are released into the air in large quantities, too much heat is trapped and the world temperature could rise. This is known as global warming.

Photochemical smog – a brownish haze that usually occurs over cities during hot, sunny weather when a mixture of air pollutants, particularly from cars, reacts with sunlight. This creates a poisonous gas called ozone that can cause breathing problems.

Radiation – a way of transferring energy from one place to another, usually by rays.

Radioactivity – a natural occurrence resulting from the breakdown of unstable atoms, which are the tiny particles that all matter is made up of. Radioactivity consists of rays or particles even tinier than atoms. Although some types of radioactivity are useful, others are damaging to living things and can stay dangerous for thousands of years.

Solvent – a substance that can dissolve other materials, like water or either. Some chemical solvents are used in paint thinners, which make paint easier to apply. Glues also contain solvents to dissolve the substances that give the glue its sticking power. Solvents get into the air when these products are used.

INDEX

Photographic Credits:
Cover and pages 10, 12, 15 bottom, 19, 21 top and middle, 22 right, 28 and 29 top: Frank Spooner Pictures; pages 4-5: Roger Vlitos; pages 6, 11 bottom, 12-13, 16 right and 22 left: The Robert Harding Picture Library; pages 7 and 14: Planet Earth Pictures; pages 9 and 29 bottom: Science Photo Library; pages 11 top, 20, 21 bottom, 23 right and 24: Eye Ubiquitous; page 15 top: Lena Skarby; pages 16 left and 23 bottom: The Hutchison Library; page 23 left: Spectrum Colour Library.

PRINTED IN BELGIUM BY

proost
INTERNATIONAL BOOK PRODUCTION